Original title:
The Porch of Our Youth

Copyright © 2025 Creative Arts Management OÜ
All rights reserved.

Author: Franklin Stone
ISBN HARDBACK: 978-1-80587-193-4
ISBN PAPERBACK: 978-1-80587-663-2

Reflections in the Summer Rain

Puddles glisten, shoes in flight,
Jumping madly, pure delight.
Our laughter drowns out the storm,
Umbrella upside down, what a norm!

Raiders of the slippy ground,
Wipeouts turning joy quite round.
Splashing puddles, friends unite,
Carefree chaos, oh what a sight!

Fragments of Joy on the Veranda

Old rocking chairs creak with glee,
We trade tall tales of the sea.
Lemonade's dripping down our chins,
Rivalries spark, oh, let the games begin!

Cats in sunbeams take their naps,
While we plot all our funny mishaps.
Who spilled ketchup on the cat?
It's a wonder, where's he at?

Tales of Laughter and Longing

Silly hats and mismatched shoes,
Giggling fits spill out the blues.
Retreat to laughs beneath the stars,
With wishes made on silly cars.

Our secrets whispered in the night,
Moonlight dancing, pure delight.
From broken swings to wild dreams,
Life is better than it seems!

Fleeting Days of Swirling Leaves

Autumn breezes through the trees,
We dive into piles with such ease.
Squirrels scurry, we shout, "Dare!"
Leaves in the air, a playful flare.

Mischief blooms beneath the sun,
Who can catch us? Let's just run.
Each twirl brings giggles, hearts so light,
Chasing shadows, oh what a sight!

Playing Hide and Seek with Time

We chased the sun, giggles in the air,
Around the corner, with no hint of care.
Time played tricks, like a teasing breeze,
We'd shout and jump, forget our knees.

With every breath, we'd race and fall,
Counting to ten, against the old wall.
In the blink, it blurred past our eyes,
A game of bliss under wide-open skies.

Joyful Echoes of Barefoot Adventures

We dashed through fields, so wild and free,
Mud on our toes, with laughter's decree.
Daring each other to leap over streams,
Living our lives in bright, chaotic dreams.

Catching fireflies under the moon's soft grace,
Each flicker a treasure, like a warm embrace.
Barefoot glory, in summer's sweet glow,
Our hearts in sync, moving fast, then slow.

Vows Made Under Swings

Swinging high, we'd make a pact,
To rule the world, never look back.
With peanut butter and jelly on toast,
We dreamt of futures, oh, how we'd boast!

"Forever friends!" we'd laugh and shout,
On creaky swings, we had no doubt.
Our voices carried, like birds out of sight,
Planning world takeovers, under moonlight.

The Old Oak Tree Chronicles

We carved our names on the bark so stout,
Whispers of secrets, full of clout.
Adventures lived in each twisted limb,
An acorn hat to fit our whim!

With each new season, our tree would glow,
A compass of joy, instructing our flow.
Beneath its shade, we spun endless tales,
Of daring rescues and pirate sails.

Giggles in the Golden Hour

Laughter rings as shadows play,
Chasing dreams at end of day.
Spilled juice upon the ground,
Sticky hands and joy abound.

A dog named Max with fur so bright,
Chasing fireflies in the night.
We catch the stars, we drop a shoe,
Life's a laugh with much to do.

Footprints on Sun-Kissed Wood

Barefoot races, muddy toes,
Tickling grass where the river flows.
Old wooden boards creak with glee,
As we dance like ants at sea.

Silly hats and lemonade,
Sunscreen smeared—a funny trade.
Our antics bright as afternoon,
Echoes of our wild cartoon.

The Swing Between Now and Then

Swinging high and swinging low,
Time's a laugh, don't you know?
Reaching for the clouds above,
Counting clouds, oh how we love!

Hiccups shared mid-air delight,
Who can hold their breath? Not quite!
The world below spins fast and wide,
In our hearts, we take a ride.

Rivals of the Afternoon Light

Silly shadows dance and greet,
Challenge sun to a silly feat.
Falling leaves and running feet,
With giggles mixing soft and sweet.

Pranks abound and laughter rolls,
Ticklish spots, we target souls.
In sun's embrace, we spin and twirl,
Forever young, our laughter curls.

A Canvas of Dreams and Clarity

In a world made of candy, we'd laugh and we'd play,
Our bikes were rockets, zooming all day.
Chasing after fireflies, we'd giggle and shout,
As ice cream dripped down, we'd laugh it all out.

With mud on our faces, we'd race through the park,
Pretending we're heroes, shining so stark.
Daring each other to climb the tall trees,
Swinging like monkeys, just buzzing like bees.

A canvas of colors splashed all around,
Our imaginations spun wildly unbound.
Caught up in our dreams, we thought we could fly,
With wishes on balloons, we painted the sky.

We'd build up our forts from just pillows and sheets,
Inventing great stories with grand, funny feats.
And if laughter could echo, it surely would burst,
For moments like these are the ones we love first.

Where Time Stood Still for a While

Remember those days, with no worries in sight,
When sunbeams would dance, and the world felt just right?
We'd build our own kingdoms out back in the grass,
With crowns made of daisies, we'd rule over class.

Time moved like syrup, so sweet and so slow,
With secrets exchanged just behind the old row.
We'd share silly jokes that made no sense at all,
Or slip on a banana peel—oh, what a fall!

In our magic domain, we savored each snack,
Chasing away clouds with a thunderous clack.
If only we knew the minutes would flee,
We'd savor that laughter, just you and me.

As the sun sank away, painting skies a bright blue,
We'd whisper our dreams, sharing what we'd pursue.
Where tick-tock was silenced, and fun had a style,
Oh, how we danced where time stood still for a while.

Stories Woven in the Air

In the hush of the evening, we'd spin our great tales,
Of daring young pirates and wild, sailing gales.
Each laugh would be a thread, weaving bonds that we'd share,
With stories so big, they floated on air.

The tree's our great ship, sailing seas of bright dreams,
With a crew made of pals, or so it all seems.
Our swords made of sticks, we'd battle with glee,
As laughter echoed loud, just my mate and me.

We mended the world with a giggle or two,
Adventures on playgrounds, with nothing to rue.
Each moment felt grand, with keepsakes in tow,
Oh, the wild, silly places our imaginations would go.

In the twilight's embrace, where whispers took flight,
We'd cherish the tales that would dance in the night.
With stories like clouds, drifting high in the air,
The laughter we shared is forever so rare.

Nostalgic Rhythms of Becoming

On the swings we would take off, defiantly high,
Soaring over rooftops, just brushing the sky.
Every creak of the chains sang a song of delight,
As we boomeranged back, a nostalgic flight.

With sneakers untied, we'd run wild and free,
Discovery our compass, with no map for the sea.
The world was our stage, and we danced like weirdos,
Chasing imaginary cars, giggling in a row.

Once upon silly dreams, in the world of our youth,
We'd dive deep in puddles, seeking laughs and truth.
With each splash we made, we left worries behind,
A world full of whimsy, entwined and unrefined.

As shadows grew long, and the stars would appear,
We'd share all our secrets, our laughter, our cheer.
In the rhythm of time, we found joy while becoming,
Those days wrapped in laughter, forever still humming.

Choose Your Own Adventure at Twilight

We rode our bikes down the hill,
Dodging cats with a thrilling thrill.
Chasing fireflies, what a chase,
Each one wore its own sparkly grace.

In treehouses made of dreams and wood,
Pretending we were brave and good.
Mischief brewed in whispered plans,
With sticky fingers and ice cream tans.

We'd plot our escape from grown-up rules,
While planning the world with giggling fools.
Each turn a risk, each laugh a chance,
In twilight's glow, we'd dance and prance.

Oh, those evenings where for once,
We feasted on laughter and playful puns.
The stars above, our night's own guide,
As we sailed on adventures, wild and wide.

Heartbeats Within the Sweet Escape

Under the warm summer blaze,
We played our games, oh what a phase.
Jumping in puddles, splashing each prank,
To be young and wild, we drew on the bank.

Each heartbeat echoed beneath our feet,
As we danced in shoes that were way too beat.
Telling tall tales of brave knights' feats,
While dodging pesky mosquitoes' treats.

We painted our days in laughter's hue,
With spills and thrills in bright colors too.
Running through fields till summer's end,
Crafting friendships that would never bend.

As the sun dipped low, our laughter soared,
The world seemed magical, and hearts adored.
In those fleeting moments, we found our song,
Forever echoing, we could do no wrong.

Memories like Leaves, Falling Softly

Leaves painted gold began to fall,
We gathered them up, a leafy ball.
Every crunch was a sound of glee,
In a world made of crisp autumn spree.

We trapped our dreams in paper boats,
Floating them down where the river gloats.
Our wishes sailed, some wild and free,
Caught in the laughter of you and me.

With each leaf that twirled on air,
We spun our visions, unaware of care.
Fun-filled afternoons turned into night,
As darkness danced in flickering light.

Each moment woven in nature's quilt,
With silly antics and friendships built.
Like leaves that drift softly to the ground,
Our joy in those days, forever found.

The Colors of a Canvas Unseen

With crayons in hand, we drew our fate,
A scribbled world, oh so first-rate.
Sunshine and giggles splattered wide,
On canvas of dreams where laughter can hide.

We painted our worries right out of sight,
In swirls of giggles, oh what a sight!
Drawing castles in the air with flair,
Tangled in nonsense, we haven't a care.

The laughter spilled like the brightest paint,
Our wild visions had no constraint.
Each stroke a memory forever bright,
In the art of youth, we found our light.

With brush-stained hands and bruised-up knees,
We created magic, a wonderful tease.
The world, a palette of vivid hues,
With every color, we danced and we'd lose.

Morning Glory and Wildflowers

We woke up early, sun in our sights,
Sneaking cookies, oh, what sweet bites!
Laughter erupted with each silly prank,
We danced in the garden, our spirits so rank.

Chasing the butterflies, dreams in our heads,
Building our castles with soft, flowery threads.
Just kids with a giggle, a wink, and a cheer,
Time seemed to slow down, nothing to fear.

With paint on our fingers, we'd color the world,
Our laughter like ribbons, happily swirled.
We'd swing from the branches, so high, so free,
The wildflowers danced with our glee, can't you see?

Even the daisies would nod in delight,
As we raced after dreams, from morning 'til night.
With the sun on our backs, the sky so wide,
We built our adventures, hearts open with pride.

The Harmony of Youthful Hearts

With canisters of chalk, we'd tag our domain,
Sidewalk symphonies, a colorful train.
Our laughter like music, ringing so clear,
In a world of our making, we conquered our fear.

Imaginary kingdoms, we'd scuffle and scheme,
Galloping on bikes, we'd chase down a dream.
In tights made for heroes, we'd leap and we'd bound,
Each day was a concert, a jubilant sound.

Whispers and secrets, the night softly fell,
Under the stars, we spun every tale.
Stargazers clutching our hopes in a jar,
While candy-wrapped wishes drifted afar.

The harmonies echoed, our hearts beat as one,
A chorus of youth, our endless fun.
In dance and in laughter, we'd twirl 'round the park,
Singing sweet laughter till it grew dark.

Under the Canopy of Memories

Beneath the big oak, our kingdom was set,
With clubs made of sticks, we never had regret.
The laughter was magical, tales spun so grand,
With treasure maps drawn in the soft, golden sand.

We'd act like the pirates, bold strangers at sea,
Imaginary booty just waiting for thee.
But mostly our bickering would turn into fun,
With wooden swords clashing, from sun up to done.

The canopy whispered, our secrets well-kept,
From spatula heroes who always wept.
Every summer breeze sang a sweet lullaby,
While fireflies twinkled like stars in the sky.

In the branches we found our own brand of grace,
Each moment a treasure, a jubilant space.
With memories threaded like vines all around,
We built a world timeless, in laughter, profound.

Bonds That Spanned the Seasons

As spring painted flowers, we'd run in a race,
Through mud-puddled streets, with dirt on our face.
Autumn brought leaves, we'd jump in the piles,
Each laugh a confession, each moment a smile.

Winter brought snow, and snowmen we'd seek,
With scarves that seemed lost, we'd laugh until weak.
In summer, we'd splash, creating a storm,
Our hearts felt so light, carelessly warm.

Seasons would change, yet we stayed so tight,
Building our friendships beneath stars so bright.
Climbing up trees, demanding to peek,
On the adventures we had, no one could critique.

As the years waddled by, like ducks, oh so slow,
Our stories kept growing, as friendships would flow.
In the fabric of time, we wove our own thread,
With bonds that were sewn, our laughter widespread.

Silent Promises Under the Moonlight

Whispers bounced from chair to chair,
As laughter filled the humid air.
Ice cream dribbled on a shirt,
Friendships made, oh how they flirt!

Fireflies danced with glee,
While we sipped our favorite tea.
Secrets spilled with a giggle and grin,
Under the glow, the night wore thin.

The world felt big, our worries small,
As we dared each other, one and all.
With silly stories, we spun our dreams,
In sticky summer air, or so it seems.

Each promise made—our hearts would cheer,
While pranks were planned for the next year.
Under stars, we'd shout and cheer,
For in that moment, nothing could smear.

The Safety of Shadows and Sunbeams

We played hide and seek in the yard,
Ducking behind bushes, it wasn't that hard.
In halos of sunlight, we'd prance about,
While our imaginations sparked a wild shout!

Sneaking out to sample the breeze,
Chasing the laughter beneath the trees.
Silly fights, with water balloons,
And dreams of flying to the moon soon.

Shadows chased us, fluttering fast,
While we vowed this fun would forever last.
Foot races ended with grass stains galore,
And memories built like castles on shore.

In that blur of light and games,
We named our fantasies, gave them fame.
With goofy looks and playful yells,
We spun our tales only friendship tells.

Secrets Shared Beneath the Sky's Canopy

Beneath a blanket, all snug and tight,
We'd tell ghost stories, a soft-lit fright.
With popcorn battles and candy fights,
Our giggles echoed, even on cold nights.

The night sky held a million stars,
Wishing we'd all beam, like shooting cars.
Under our canvas, time flew so fast,
Who knew our childhood joy would blast?

While plotting pranks, a slip, a fall,
Belly laughs were the best of all.
Each secret shared like a precious jewel,
In the warmth of friendship, we felt so cool.

So here's to those days, so silly, so bright,
Where shadows danced in the moonlit night.
With every chuckle, we found our way,
In the garden of youth, forever we'll play.

Pages of our Journey in Dusty Light

Scraped knees spoke of daring feats,
As we raced on bikes with tangled cheats.
Old books opened, their covers cracked,
Stories in ink, our time intact.

In dusty corners where treasures lay,
We hid away secrets that sparked the day.
Fortresses built from chairs and sheets,
Each bravery tested as laughter repeats.

Our world became a stage so grand,
Where mischief ruled and love took a stand.
Carved into hearts, those moments so light,
Forever embraced in the daytime bright.

Oh, the chaos and cheer of our wild youth,
Where every slip was a search for truth.
With crayons, we colored outside the lines,
Celebrating joy that endlessly shines!

Revelry of Days Long Past

We danced on grass with wild abandon,
Laughter echoed, a jolly cannon.
Ice cream dripped down our sunny hands,
As sticky joy was all we planned.

The radio played our favorite tune,
We dived in grass, a makeshift lagoon.
Big hats and shades, a fashion spree,
What trend we started! Oh, can't you see?

Bicycles raced, the wind took flight,
We painted dreams in colors bright.
Our voices soared like birds in play,
In moments lost, where we used to sway.

Now we chuckle at those skies we chased,
With every slip, our pride displaced.
A time capsule of gone-to-sea,
Oh, how we thrived in youthful glee!

The Garden of Our Unwritten Stories

In a garden where wild tales were sown,
We spun our dreams, free as windblown.
Each flower a secret, buried deep,
In laughter's soil, our memories creep.

Kites flew high, crinkled noses wide,
Over fences, imagination would slide.
We fought with swords made of curved sticks,
Our heroic tales full of kid's tricks.

The sun cast spells on our giggly crew,
As we ventured forth, never a clue.
With backyard mysteries to unfold,
Our hearts embraced the mischief bold.

Now we laugh at the chaos we wrought,
In that garden where friendship was sought.
Those unwritten stories, forever bright,
In pages unwritten, still take flight.

Footprints in the Dust of Tomorrow

We raced the sun, our shadows in tow,
With every jump, the world was aglow.
It's hard to tell if we were too brave,
Or just reckless kids who danced with a wave.

Sandy toes and giggles in the breeze,
Our footprints etched with such careless ease.
From flip-flops flying to laughter loud,
We made mischief, made our heads proud.

Those days of sun, splashes, and cheer,
Surrounded by friends, what could we fear?
Time became silly, a looped old track,
We never looked forward, never looked back.

Yet here we are, with smiles that still bloom,
Remembering the mischief that danced in the room.
Our footprints mark what tomorrow may lend,
In this life's race, we'll always pretend.

Echoes of Secrets Beneath the Eaves

Beneath the eaves, where whispers grew,
We hatched our plots in a huddle of two.
Silly schemes and plans never clear,
Yet laughter carried, ever near.

A treehouse kingdom, our lofty throne,
With snack-time feasts, we'd munch on our own.
Hidden treasures in pockets of dreams,
Each secret shared sparked our wild schemes.

Echoes of giggles in late evening light,
Our tales grew tall, a playful fright.
Stories of monsters beneath the bed,
Only for brave hearts, yet we were led.

As years rolled on, those echoes remain,
A symphony sweet, with joy and with pain.
We craft our tales, beneath life's grand eaves,
Forever young, as long as one believes.

Echoes of Playtime Adventures

We climbed the trees with ice cream in hand,
Chasing our dreams on soft, golden sand.
Laughter rang out like a melody sweet,
We danced around, with bare, joyful feet.

The sun kissed our skin, so bright and so bold,
Trading our secrets, our stories retold.
Those silly mishaps, like tripping on shoes,
Are treasures of fun in the life that we choose.

With funny faces at dolls that we made,
Our giggles erupted, our worries just fade.
We ruled the whole world from swings up so high,
With dreams in our pockets, we'd never say die.

So here's to our laughter, our silly young games,
To friendship that sparkles like wild, fiery flames.
In echoes of playtime our spirits will soar,
Forever united, we'll cherish and roar!

Between Moments of Laughter and Sorrow

We'd laugh till we cried, then cry till we laughed,
With pranks just as wild as the best comic draft.
In every mischief, in every small scheme,
We found playful joy in each fleeting dream.

Like flowers in bloom on a warm summer's day,
We'd dance in the sun, letting worries decay.
Between ice cream spills and silly rough fights,
Friendship became our delight through the nights.

There's humor in failures, and wisdom in fun,
In races to nowhere, our hearts would yet run.
The hide-and-seek games always led to the best,
In moments of joy, we discovered our zest.

So let's raise a toast with our old, chipped cups,
With giggles and smiles, we're never grown-ups.
For in the bittersweet that life may unearth,
We find endless laughter, worth more than its worth!

The Sun-Drenched Pathways of Us

We'd sprint down the walk in a wild summer race,
With bubbles and giggles that danced on our face.
Sun-kissed and carefree, we played till the night,
Our paths shone like stars in the fading twilight.

Epic bike rides that ended with falls,
That left us both laughing, with bruises and sprawls.
We'd build up our castles from sand on the beach,
With dreams that were massive, just out of our reach.

Caught stealing cookies when Grandma looked away,
With crumbs on our shirts, we would giggle and sway.
Each adventure a treasure, no matter how small,
In sun-drenched days, we'd conquer it all.

So let's put on our shoes and revisit those lanes,
Where memories linger like soft summer rains.
With laughter as compass, our hearts will still trust,
In the sun-drenched pathways, forever with us!

Spaces of Joy Between Yesterday and Tomorrow

In the spaces of time where fun never ends,
We'd dream up new games with our very best friends.
With silly inventions and wacky new plans,
We'd conquer the world with our cartoonish stands.

Like shadows at dusk, we played tag with the sun,
Creating wild stories, our hearts filled with fun.
With friendship as fuel for our joyful delight,
We'd laugh through the day, then stargaze at night.

Tales of mishaps would echo in glee,
As we rolled down the hill, just carefree and free.
Trading our secrets, like marbles we swapped,
With giggles still ringing, we'd never be stopped.

So here's to the moments of joy ever bright,
In the spaces between, where everything's right.
With laughter as magic, the future we'll claim,
In memories crafted, we'll cherish our name!

Dancing Feet and Dreaming Souls

We twirled in circles, like socks on the floor,
Chasing after giggles, who could ask for more?
With pizza on our faces, we danced till we dropped,
Each leap a new laugh, we just couldn't stop.

The neighbors all stared, shaking heads in delight,
As we launched into moves under soft porch light.
Our shadows grew long, but our spirits stayed high,
Like our ice cream cones, we'd just never die!

Who knew our two left feet would lead us to fame?
The porch became magic, not just a plain frame.
We invented wild games, no need for a chart,
In our kingdom of laughter, we played from the heart.

So here's to those days, when the world felt so grand,
Where friendship and fun go hand in hand.
We'd wear mismatched shoes, our attire quite bold,
In the archives of youth, our stories unfold.

The Lightness of Being Unbound

We skipped with our shadows, like bubbles in air,
Wore crowns made of leaves, without a single care.
Our laughter was music, a bright joyful sound,
Oh, how it felt light, like we'd never touch ground!

A squirrel would chime in, with his chatter so loud,
Claiming the throne as the star of the crowd.
We'd mimic the birds, with our tongues in a twist,
Trying to soar with a comedic twist!

With lemonade spills and temporary pets,
Our mishaps made legends, with no regrets yet.
A dance-off with bugs, on our whimsical stage,
The audience of ants, cheering louder with age!

So here's to our shenanigans, wild and free,
Where kids lost in giggles can climb any tree.
Identities crafted from dreams and our cheer,
In that timeless moment, we felt so sincere.

Reflecting on the Joyful Melodies

We'd sing silly tunes, off-key but with pride,
With makeshift bandmates, we'd never subside.
Instruments fashioned from old pots and pans,
Our jams were a festival; the whole world danced!

We'd serenade dusk with our cacophony sweet,
As fireflies flickered, grooving to our beat.
A chorus of laughter, each lyric a jest,
In our grand concert, all friends were the best.

The air full of jokes, we'd whisper and scheme,
Crafting more pranks than a kid's wildest dream.
The harmony of chaos, we laughed till we cried,
With the echo of joy, we felt so alive!

So let's raise a glass to the songs we once sung,
To those melted ice creams and the friends that we've flung.
In this dance of remembrance, we still reign supreme,
Forever young at heart, living life like a dream.

The Garden of Our Secret Dreams

Underneath the tree so grand,
We planted thoughts, just hand in hand.
Beneath the blooms, we laughed so loud,
Wishing for clouds that looked like a cow.

The daisies told us silly jokes,
While squirrels danced in bunny cloaks.
Each sunbeam caught our youthful cheer,
Our giggles echoing far and near.

We gathered whispers from the breeze,
Swapping secrets with the buzzing bees.
A garden filled with hopes and dreams,
Where nothing's ever as it seems.

In muddy shoes, our sketches drawn,
Chasing sunsets until the dawn.
In every petal, a story spun,
A tapestry of laughter won.

Cherished Moments Beneath the Stars

With our heads upon the grassy floor,
We counted stars and wanted more.
Each blink above seemed like a wink,
As we whispered secrets, both bold and pink.

We crafted wishes like paper boats,
Sailing dreams on moonlit moats.
Shooting stars played hide and seek,
While we burst out laughing, what a cheek!

The Milky Way was our disco ball,
We twirled around, we'd never fall.
In the dark, we felt so free,
Like kittens chasing after a bumblebee.

Each twinkle held a silly jest,
"Do they see us?" we'd often jest.
Oh, to be young, with hearts aglow,
Under the night's fantastic show.

A Symphony of Crickets and Dreams

In twilight's soft and cozy hum,
Crickets played tunes as day was done.
Each chirp a chuckle, sweet and bright,
While we plotted pranks throughout the night.

With jars of fireflies as our lights,
We danced and tumbled, reaching heights.
Imagined worlds behind each sound,
Where silly shenanigans abound.

We'd build a fort from leaves and sticks,
Creating magic with our little tricks.
In every hiccup, each sudden pause,
Were echoes of joy, loud applause.

The crickets laughed, we joined in too,
Our youthful giggles were quite the crew.
In dreams we soared, in laughter we basked,
With nature our stage, we simply masked.

Shadows Cast by Fading Light

As shadows lengthened, we made our masks,
Imitating adults with comical tasks.
We debated on who had the best sway,
Like goofy giants at the end of the day.

Beneath the sunset's golden hue,
We posed for pictures, a silly crew.
We painted our faces with berry stains,
Laughing at life without any chains.

In the twilight breeze, our laughter soared,
As fading daylight softly implored.
We chased our shadows, round and round,
Creating memories that knew no bound.

At dusk we turned to jesters bright,
In our kingdom of fading light.
With every moment a treasure to keep,
A playful heart, a joy so deep.

Where Innocence Met Forever

We built a fort from sofa chairs,
With chocolate snacks, our secret layers.
A kingdom ruled by giggles loud,
In our brave hearts, we both felt proud.

The garden hose became a stream,
We sailed our ships on foamy dreams.
With mud-stained knees and wild hair,
Adventure beckoned everywhere.

A slingshot aimed at glow bugs' glow,
Each failed shot caused our laughter's flow.
We tangled toes in dew-soaked grass,
As sunlight made our worries pass.

Then came the time to say goodbye,
With zany plans and silly sighs.
But in our minds, we'll still reside,
In laughter's joy, our hearts will bide.

Navigating the River of Time's Embrace

A paper boat made from a snack,
We'd race it down the hallway track.
With pirate hats from mom's old cap,
We swore we'd never take a nap.

We caught the rain in our own cups,
As puddles formed like messy hiccups.
In stealthy moves, we danced around,
While mischief made the best of sounds.

The clock would tick, but we'd pretend,
Each moment stretched, we'd never end.
With bubblegum and broken rules,
In our own world, we were the fools.

To dream of spaceships made from straws,
Our laughter the only sound that draws.
In time's embrace, we'll always find,
Those silly days so sweetly kind.

The Unwritten Chapters of Carefree Days

We crafted stories with new crayons,
Of daring knights and giant crayons.
Each page a canvas, bright and bold,
In laughter's ink, our tales were told.

We drew our treasure maps with flair,
In search of sweets beyond compare.
A cookie quest through endless fields,
The joy we found was truth revealed.

Cartwheels spun like our wild dreams,
We'd tumble down in fitful screams.
With daring leaps from garden walls,
The echoes of our youth, our calls.

When sunsets marked our playful time,
We'd sneak a candy bar, sublime.
In unwritten chapters, joy remains,
In every line, the fun sustains.

Threads of Laughter in the Wind

We wove our stories on a breeze,
With leaves that danced among the trees.
Each laugh a thread pulled tight and strong,
In nature's choir, we sung along.

The wind would carry our silly rhymes,
As hopscotch became a game of crimes.
A chase for ice cream dripped away,
With sticky hands to mark the day.

Our whispers flew like dandelions,
Creating dreams of wild designs.
With popsicle stains on summer skin,
Every adventure sparked within.

So here we stand, in childish glee,
With threads of laughter, wild and free.
In memory's fabric tight and grand,
Forever young, hand in hand.

A Tapestry of Timeless Laughter

In the sun, we danced with glee,
Our feet caught in a funny spree.
With ice cream drips on shirts so bright,
We raced the cats, oh what a sight!

We told tall tales beneath the tree,
Of haunted socks and a dancing flea.
With giggles shared, time would elude,
The world was ours, wild and crude.

Our voices bounced like bouncy balls,
Through laughter that would fill the halls.
Chasing shadows in the park,
We built our dreams, from dawn 'til dark.

So here we stand, a motley crew,
With silly hats and a pet goldfish too.
We age but keep that spark alive,
In memories where we still thrive.

Unraveled Dreams in the Golden Hour

Golden rays through branches tease,
While we giggle in the summer breeze.
With flip-flops flying, we race the sun,
Our laughter echoing, so much fun!

Beneath the swings, we plot our schemes,
Of grand adventures, silly dreams.
With lemonade mustaches, we claim our throne,
In our kingdom of cushions, we're never alone.

A wooden fort, made of twine,
Where secret plans and snacks align.
We armed with smiles and humor divine,
In our minds, we're heroes by design.

The clock ticks on, but we don't mind,
For in this bliss, all joys unwind.
Together still, we laugh and play,
In hearts, forever young we stay.

Innocent Hearts Under the Canopy

Underneath the leafy shade,
We chased the squirrels, how they played!
With secret codes and rubber bands,
We fashioned dreams from playground lands.

Ice-cold limonade in the sun,
With sticky hands, we'd just begun.
We dared the sky to rain or shine,
Painting worlds with dreams divine.

Our laughter echoed through the trees,
As we climbed high, swaying with ease.
Falling down was just pure glee,
With dirt on our cheeks, we were wild and free.

Sunset skies with hues so bright,
We spun tales till we lost the light.
With goofy grins and hearts ablaze,
In every moment, we found our ways.

The Garden Wall of Yesteryears' Roots

In a garden where laughter blooms,
We planted seeds with silly fumes.
With wiggly worms in our pockets deep,
We danced around till we fell asleep.

The fence was built with broken dreams,
Of fairy tales and saucy themes.
We'd trade our toys for secret maps,
Where every path led to silly mishaps.

With ladybugs as our little friends,
We fought off monsters at garden bends.
In tiny forts of leaves and sticks,
We spun our tales with magic tricks.

So wander back to those bright days,
With vivid smiles and playful ways.
For in our hearts, those moments thrived,
In a garden where joy survived.

The Creaks and Cracks of Growing Up

We climbed so high on wobbly chairs,
With stories wound up in tangled hair.
Falling off was part of the show,
Yet laughter echoed through each ebb and flow.

We played with dreams of who we'd be,
While eating snacks that stuck like glue.
The creaks were songs of our own delight,
As time spun tales beneath the moonlight.

Every step felt like a grand mistake,
Knees scraped down from the swings we make.
With friends who blur in a giggling race,
Growing up was just a silly phase.

We waved goodbye with sticky hands,
To a world of wonders and befuddled plans.
In those days, we danced like fools,
With creaks and cracks that made the rules.

Sundrenched Moments in Our Imaginings

Under clouds made of candyfloss,
We spun around, feeling like the boss.
With sun-kissed cheeks and silly grins,
Each day was new, that's how it begins.

Inventing games in our own domain,
With homemade crowns, we took the reign.
Sundrenched laughter lit the air,
As we plotted mischief without a care.

Hiding from chores was our grand plan,
We'd paint the world with a magic crayon.
Each sunset brought a quest anew,
Chasing dreams in every shade of blue.

With sticky fingers and wild cheers,
We built our castle from grand ideas.
In those moments, we felt so alive,
Where every second made our spirits thrive.

The Rustle of Leaves and Untold Adventures

Amidst the whispers of branches sway,
Our feet would dance, come what may.
With tree forts stacked to dizzying heights,
We crafted worlds with our imaginations' flights.

The rustle of leaves sang secret calls,
As we clambered and stumbled over the walls.
Adventures lived in hidden nooks,
Where every turn offers leaps like books.

Our laughter echoed 'neath the sky,
As we chased dreams that fluttered by.
Untold tales filled every shout,
With whispers of fun that left no doubt.

From treasure hunts in the backyard zone,
To fairy tales we claimed as our own.
The nights spoke to us, wild and free,
Saying, "These adventures were meant to be!

Chasing Fireflies in the Softening Grayscale

As daylight faded to a gentle hush,
We darted out in a gleeful rush.
Chasing fireflies with hearts aglow,
In the softening dusk, our laughter would flow.

In shades of gray, our giggles took flight,
With every spark, we felt pure delight.
The world was a canvas, painted in dreams,
As echoes of joy danced in moonbeams.

We raced through grass, bare feet in tow,
With mischief brewing, we let it show.
Each glow a hope, each flicker a chance,
In our little world, we'd twirl and prance.

When darkness fell, the magic nestled tight,
We whispered secrets to stars so bright.
Chasing after flickers, we found our grace,
In those moments, time ceased its race.

Echoes of Innocence Lost

We raced our bikes down winding streets,
With wobbly wheels and messy feats.
Chasing ice cream trucks, oh what a thrill,
Till someone yelled, 'It's time to chill!'

With sticky hands and silly grins,
We plotted schemes where no one wins.
Hiding from grown-ups, what a delight,
Only to trip on a dog at night.

We made up stories, so grand, so wild,
Of dragons and treasures, like a bold child.
Yet somehow, we lost the playful spark,
Now stories live only in the dark.

Summer Shadows and Laughter

Sunshine beams through swaying trees,
We'd laugh so hard, we'd beg for ease.
Hide-and-seek in the backyard flair,
Landing in bushes, with leaves in hair.

We climbed tall fences, felt like kings,
Impersonating birds on wiry swings.
But still, that dreaded call rang true,
'Time for dinner!'—what a hullabaloo!

Wet swimsuits and daisy chains,
Running through sprinklers, laughing in rains.
Those carefree days, oh how they sped,
Yet all that echoes now is what we said.

Memories in the Gentle Breeze

In the warm sun, we played for hours,
Turning weeds into epic flowers.
We'd make bold wishes on birthday cakes,
And race the wind without any brakes.

With mischievous grins, we'd plot and plan,
To sneak into drapes like a stealthy clan.
But then we'd giggle, caught in our deed,
Hiding behind while planting a seed.

Granny's stories of pirates so grand,
In those myths, we took our stand.
Now those tales just float on by,
Like dandelions lost to the sky.

Where Dreams Took Flight

We'd craft our dreams from bits of string,
Building castles fit for a king.
Armed with crayons, we'd color the day,
Unlocking wonders in our own way.

We climbed tall trees like dizzy squirrels,
In our secret world, we'd give it twirls.
But when the moon peeked over the street,
It was time to retreat, oh, bittersweet!

With fluffy clouds as our feathered planes,
We flew so high, ignoring the rains.
Now those flights are just tales to be told,
Each laugh a gem we now cherish as gold.

Footsteps in the Grass of Yesterday

We ran with laughter, barefoot and bold,
Chasing the shadows that the day would hold.
In tangled weeds, we lost our shoes,
And wandered around, without a clue.

With ice cream drips on our sun-kissed faces,
We mapped our dreams in secret places.
Falling down, we'd roll in mirth,
Creating chaos that rocked our earth.

Age was a number, we laughed at time,
Balancing jokes on a crooked rhyme.
We played like kings on an unseen throne,
Inventing worlds that we'd call our own.

Footsteps fade, but memories stick,
Like the taste of sugar from a sweetened trick.
With silly grins, we claimed our past,
In a sunny patch, our joys held fast.

Dancing with Fireflies in Dusk

Glowing lights twinkled, a magical show,
We spun 'round and 'round, putting on a glow.
Waving our arms like we were true stars,
Stumbling over each other, with the world on Mars.

Laughter erupted as we fell in a heap,
Like rising bread dough, we'd bounce and leap.
With each little blink of the bugs in flight,
We'd catch fleeting moments wrapped up in night.

A dance floor of dirt, with fireflies we chased,
In the pockets of dusk, we flittered and raced.
The world dimmed down, but our spirits soared,
In a wobbly waltz, we never were bored.

When morning comes, who'll recall the thrill?
Just our giggles, resounding still.
With each glowing bug, a memory stirs,
In vibrant dreams, forever ours.

Secrets Shared in Soft Glows

Whispers danced in the twilight air,
We shared our secrets without a care.
With shadows looming, we huddled close,
Creating a bond no one would oppose.

Giggles muffled, under blankets tight,
Piecing together our fears of the night.
A treasure chest filled with hopes and dreams,
We traded tales and silly memes.

In the soft glow of our makeshift fire,
We swore such promises would never tire.
From dreams of jelly beans to flying high,
We painted the sky with our hopes up high.

And though the years may stretch like a string,
We'll carry our secrets like flowers in spring.
In the heart of laughter, our stories will stay,
Reflecting the joy of our youthful play.

The Pulse of Unbreakable Bonds

With silly pranks that we played all day,
Our goofy antics kept worries at bay.
Like gum on our shoes, we stuck like glue,
Crafting a friendship that blossomed anew.

We'd race through the fields, tripping on grass,
Celebrating each tumble, oh how we'd laugh!
In our hat of tricks, we lived so grand,
With whispers of mischief beautifully planned.

Filling the air with soaked-up giggles,
As we boiled with joy that made us wiggle.
Through all of our stumbles, we'll never part,
For laughter's the beat that connects our hearts.

So when the world shifts and we grow old,
Our friendship's the treasure, forever bold.
In the kaleidoscope of time, our song,
Will pulse like a heartbeat, forever strong.

Nostalgic Moments in the Twilight Hues

Once we chased fireflies, hands in the air,
With laughter that echoed, like we had no care.
Ice cream dripped down our chins, what a sight!
My brother's wild dance gave the evening its light.

We'd build grand forts with sheets and some chairs,
Conjuring castles, complete with wild stares.
Dad would peek in, bearing popcorn so warm,
We'd feast like kings, dreaming up tales to charm.

Hide and seek turned into an endless delight,
Cousins all giggled as we played through the night.
With every "I found you!" came new fits of glee,
Our youthful shenanigans forever carefree.

As the shadows grew long, we'd retreat with a grin,
Spinning sun-soaked tales, maps marked with where we'd been.
Those silly small moments, a treasure we kept,
Stories we shared, on adventures we leapt.

Soft Lullabies of Ages Gone By

Quiet nights echoed with whispers of dreams,
While the stars laughed softly, their glittering beams.
Mom would sing gently, her voice like a breeze,
While we'd count sheep jumping over the trees.

Old toys in the corner still gathered their dust,
As we created worlds where kindness was a must.
Teddy bears held secrets, and dolls wore their crowns,
While we ruled our kingdoms, pretending with frowns.

Running through sprinklers, rainbows would twirl,
We'd fashion our adventures, just boys and a girl.
Imaginary pirates on ships built of dreams,
With treasure maps drawn in bright colored schemes.

As we sipped on our Kool-Aid beneath the moonlight,
The world seemed to pause, just our laughter in flight.
Those lullabies linger, in times yet so clear,
Reminders of youth, forever held dear.

Breezes of Freedom and Unbridled Joy

Dirt bikes and laughter, the wind in our hair,
We raced down the street without a single care.
Worrying 'bout nothing, just chasing the sun,
With every wild turn, our spirits would run.

Piggyback rides home, mixed with bubbles and sparks,
We'd weave tales of heroes, defending our parks.
The skies felt like pastel, painted with glee,
As we swung high on swings, declaring we're free.

Water balloon fights left us soaked to the bone,
With giggles and splashes, we claimed the turf throne.
And a game of tag turned into a mad chase,
As we dashed 'round the yard, through every green space.

Those carefree moments stuck like glue to our hearts,
Whirling through time, can we savor the parts?
With breezes of laughter, so sweet on our cheeks,
We danced through the twilight, so bright, so unique.

Whispers of Sunlit Days

Sun-kissed afternoons, where the shadows would play,
We'd tumble and roll, laughing every long day.
Chasing our dreams 'neath the wide-open sky,
With imaginations soaring, together we'd fly.

Home in the evening, the scent of a feast,
With tales of our triumphs, we'd share like a feast.
Pancakes stacked high, syrup oozing so sweet,
We'd plot our next adventure, with food and with heat.

Naps turned to giggles, tucked in tight like a hug,
Where shadows danced softly, snug as a bug.
Falling asleep, the day's laughter still spun,
Those whispers of joy, brighter than the sun.

Every moment captured, like a photo frame,
We'd tell our wild stories, never quite the same.
In the quilt of our youth, stitched with love and play,
Those whispers still linger, come what may.

The Echoes of Childhood on the Steps

We played at the edge, where the shadows stretch wide,
Our laughter a river, our secrets we'd hide.
With sticks as our swords, we battled the night,
Inventing grand tales, oh what a delight!

The old wooden steps, a throne we would claim,
As kings and as queens, we'd whittle our names.
Sneaking the snacks from the kitchen behind,
With crumbs on our faces, we'd never mind!

Racing the sun as it dipped from the sky,
Frolicking freely, not one care was nigh.
The echo of giggles still lingers on air,
In the heart of our souls, we forever declare.

So here's to the youth, our wild carefree play,
Where the steps held our dreams at the end of the day.
With every mischief, we made memories sweet,
Laughter resonant, like a playful heartbeat.

Sunbeams Dancing on Our Bare Feet

Sunbeams swirled down, tickling our toes,
We raced on the grass, where the wildflower grows.
In a world made of wonder, we leaped and we spun,
With giggles like music, we basked in the sun.

The water hose drizzled a mischievous shower,
As we squealed in delight—Ah! Nature's power!
Jumping through rainbows, with our hands in the air,
Each splash an adventure, who'd have thought we'd dare!

Bare feet on the pavement, oh what a fine day,
We'd dance like wild foxes, with joy in our play.
Caught up in the chase, one foot at a time,
Our hearts beating loud in this sweet summer rhyme.

With skies dressed in blue and laughter for free,
Our world barely noticed, just you and just me.
As long as the sun casts a glow on our dreams,
We'll dance through the hours, or so it seems!

A Symphony of Giggles at Dusk

As twilight unfurls, we gather round tight,
A symphony squeals, oh what a delight!
With shadows as partners, we whirl in a spin,
While fireflies twinkle, inviting us in.

Our voices like music, a chorus of cheer,
Each note filled with mischief, our laughter sincere.
The great big oak tree, our stage for the night,
As kings and as jesters, we chortle with fright!

We'll tell ghostly tales, with a shiver and shrug,
While hiding in corners, beneath the warm rug.
With marshmallows toasted, and stories we weave,
In this twilight magic, our hearts will believe.

Oh, each silly face, each outrageous sound,
Builds a treasure of memories, so joyously found.
We'll carry this laughter, as dusk turns to night,
In the symphony of youth, everything feels right.

Lanterns of Reflection in Twilight's Embrace

In the dusky twilight, our lanterns aglow,
We sit hand in hand, with stories to throw.
The sparks fill the air, like dreams on the wing,
Each flicker a memory, each smile a spring.

We'll whisper old tales of the giggles we shared,
Of silly antics, and how much we dared.
With each little flame, we've never felt small,
In the warmth of our laughter, we've conquered it all.

The universe twirling, we dance in delight,
As shadows grow long, and stars peek at night.
With every reflection, a gleam in our eyes,
Our past filled with joy, our future a prize.

So here's to the lanterns, the stories so bright,
To the echoes of youth that will never take flight.
Together we cherish these moments, that's clear,
For within every giggle, our hearts will adhere.

A Place to Dream and Wonder

We sat on steps with ice cream in hand,
Telling tall tales, we made our own land.
A dog would bark, a cat would chase,
We laughed till we fell, in that sunny place.

With dreams so big, we reached for the sky,
Pretending to soar, wings flapping high.
Our laughter echoed, a sweet serenade,
Time slipped away like a playful charade.

The grass was our stage, the world our glee,
Every dandelion was a wish, you see?
We twirled and we danced, unashamed of the fun,
Our hearts like puzzle pieces, fitting as one.

As shadows grew longer, the sun took its bow,
We chased fireflies, made up rules on the how.
With whispers of secrets, we shared as we played,
Echoes of childhood, in memories laid.

Wandering Souls in the Warmth

Underneath the big oak, where time stood still,
We formed a club, oh what a thrill!
Sneaking snacks and giggles, oh what a bliss,
Pinky swears sealed secrets, all things amiss.

We plotted grand schemes on who'd steal a kiss,
And acted like ninjas, no shadow is amiss.
With capes made of towels, we saved the day,
Invisible forces led us astray.

The sun painted pictures, bright colors unfurled,
We built our own kingdom, the best in the world.
With swords made of sticks, our legends would grow,
We battled fierce dragons, just so you know.

As twilight approached, the stars gave a show,
We whispered our dreams, oh where would we go?
With hearts full of laughter, our spirits ran free,
Wandering souls, in childhood's decree.

Echoes of First Loves and Heartbeats

On the corner of dreams, where wishes collide,
Two hearts skipped a beat, neither dared to hide.
A glance, a giggle, oh how sweet the game,
Innocent blushes, who'd dare name the flame?

With secret exchanges, notes folded with care,
We played silly games, unaware of the dare.
Each heartbeat echoed, in whispers and sighs,
Surely the world was just us and the skies.

The hedges became curtains for our silly acts,
As we painted ourselves in mysterious facts.
The playground a stage, laughter was our tune,
We danced under stars, our hearts like the moon.

But kid's foolish dramas had a sneaky way,
Of turning sweet moments into a foul play.
With a flash of jealousy, the magic grew dim,
Yet each little moment, we held on a whim.

Lullabies of Togetherness

In the twilight glow, we sang songs of cheer,
Counting stars above, in the space we held dear.
With crayons scribbling dreams on a canvas so wide,
We painted our lives with colors inside.

Sharing our stories, a riot of glee,
It seemed our laughter was the key.
With shadow puppets, we created delight,
A zoo of the night, in whispers so light.

Cuddled in blanket forts, we faced all our fears,
With popcorn in hand, we banished the tears.
Each giggle a lullaby, soothing the night,
Our tiny adventures, a heartwarming sight.

As dreams wrapped around us, soft and secure,
We shared our wild tales that made us endure.
In our bubble of joy, we found timeless bliss,
A melody of friendship that none could dismiss.

Embracing the Endless Summer

We played tag with the sunlight bright,
Chasing dreams into the fading light.
A broken swing that squeaked with glee,
We'd laugh and tumble, wild, carefree.

Fried chicken crumbs caught in our hair,
As sticky hands gripped warm summer air.
With lemonades squirted at mischievous foes,
We danced in circles, no one knows.

Flip-flops flapping, we raced the breeze,
Hiding from chores like a well-used tease.
Fantastical tales spun from our lips,
We built our dreams on imaginary ships.

And though those days now flutter and fade,
Laughter still echoes in memories made.
With each passing cloud, we'll always find,
That endless summer lingers in our mind.

Serenading Memory in the Afternoon

Pickles and peanut butter, a savory delight,
Two hungry kids in a sunbeam's light.
We'd sing to the hedges, each note out of tune,
With ice cream cones melting far too soon.

The days stretched long, adventures galore,
Under the old oak, we begged for more.
Monsters and fairies in a game of pretend,
Where did the time go? When will it end?

Catching fireflies in jars, we would dream,
Plotting our worlds for the afternoon gleam.
With pirate hats made from our mom's old sheets,
We conquered the yard with sticky cold treats.

Though the sun may set on those days so sweet,
In our hearts, we carry those summer feats.
And when we find ourselves back from the race,
We'll serenade memories, leaving a trace.

Golden Hours of Carefree Souls

Sandy toes and giggles galore,
We'd bury each other, a heap on the shore.
Seashells our treasures, we'd proudly collect,
Each find a fortune, what did you expect?

On the grass, we sprawled like kings on their thrones,
Causing chaos, and ignoring our phones.
A lemonade fountain gave way to a fight,
With every splash, we were pure delight!

The sun dipped low, painting skies with flair,
In those golden hours, nothing could compare.
We danced in silly moves, whatever came along,
A symphony of laughter, our own silly song.

Time, a runaway kite lost in the air,
But we caught the moments without a care.
So here we stand, with smiles unrolled,
In this treasure chest of youth, we are bold.

The Tides of Innocent Laughter

Down by the creek, we found our way,
Making mischief in a grand display.
With mud on our hands and grass on our knees,
We giggled at the world, living with ease.

Water balloons launched like rainbow frisbees,
Squeals of delight carried on the breeze.
A game of hide-and-seek turned encore,
In our secret world, no worries to score.

As dusk crept in with a tinge of gold,
We shared our dreams, both daring and bold.
Creating castles from crumbs of the past,
In the tides of laughter, our spirits were cast.

So here we stand, ages lost in the tide,
Together forever, with giggles as our guide.
For those innocent hours, oh how they flew,
In the sweetest embrace, we always grew.

Whispers of Laughter Beneath the Stars

We'd gather close with snacks in hand,
Sharing tales that were oh-so grand.
A dot on the map of our crazy spree,
Imagining future adventures so free.

With glow-in-the-dark stars stuck to the ceiling,
Our giggles would echo, happiness revealing.
Each shadow danced, a playful prank,
As we painted our youth in colors that clank.

The dog wore a hat, just for sheer fun,
Chasing fireflies under the setting sun.
With whispering winds that tickled our feet,
We'd dream up a world where life felt sweet.

So, here's to the nights that stole our breath,
To laughter so loud it almost meant death.
With our hearts full of joy and hair in a mess,
We scribbled our stories, I must confess.

Shadows of Innocence in Evening Light

A jump rope twisted, we flew like the breeze,
With laughter erupting as we fell to our knees.
Imagination soared, the sky was our friend,
Creating worlds with no need to pretend.

The ice cream truck's music rang out like a bell,
We dashed to the road, as our hearts started to swell.
Sticky fingers, and faces smeared,
Were signs of the joy that we boldly endeared.

Hide-and-seek turned into a wild, funny chase,
Trying to catch shadows, we flew in our race.
Evening's glow draped us, golden and bright,
As we spun stories with magical delight.

And so, in the twilight, we we'd laugh 'til we cried,
With secrets and whispers that twinkled inside.
These moments of mischief, forever we'll keep,
As time flies away, like dreams played in sleep.

Memories Woven in Summer Breezes

In summer's embrace, we'd dance on the lawn,
With grass-stains and giggles greeting the dawn.
Our treasure maps led to the unknown,
With X marking spots where wild weeds had grown.

Water balloon battles—who knew they'd explode?
Every splash was a cheer, as we lightened our load.
With pop-sicles melting and sticky delight,
We laughed till we dropped under stars shining bright.

A cardboard spaceship built from our dreams,
We soared through the cosmos, or so it seemed.
In our imaginary worlds of candy and cheer,
Reality faded while giggles drew near.

So here's to the moments we can't quite recall,
To laughter and joy, we had it all.
Each thread of our youth woven tight in our hearts,
We stay forever young, where the magic still starts.

Where Dreams Took Flight and Blossomed

On rickety swings, we'd soar in the air,
The shouts of our joy a sweet, playful flare.
Imagining castles and dragons to tame,
As we boldly declared that life was our game.

Chasing the night with our flashlights aglow,
We'd whisper our plans where only stars could know.
Catching wishes, we'd giggle at fate,
As the moon winked down, telling us to wait.

With bicycles racing towards summer's embrace,
The wind in our hair put smiles on our face.
Splashes in puddles would echo our cheer,
In the laughter of youth, we found love without fear.

So dance with the shadows, and sing with the light,
For dreams that we harbored are still in our sight.
In echoes of laughter that never die out,
We treasure our youth, and we'll forever shout.

Melodies Carried by the Evening Breeze

Under the stars, we played our tunes,
Singing off-key to the light of the moon.
Laughter floated like fireflies near,
Who knew our voices could bring such cheer?

With crumbs of cookies and soda in hand,
We danced like no one could understand.
Each twirl was a stumble, each glide was a fall,
But we shook it off, we were having a ball.

The neighbor's cat gave us quite the glare,
As we serenaded to the night air.
We thought we were stars, a real rock band,
With a wiggle and giggle, we took our stand.

Breezes carried our secrets away,
Wrapped in the giggles of a sunny day.
In every rustle, there was our jest,
Memories stuck like glitter on the chest.

The Canvas of Our Youthful Days

With splashes of paint and brushes askew,
We made a mess of every hue.
Our fingers multicolored, our clothes like rags,
The masterpiece fled while we chased wag flags.

We painted the grass, our legs a deep green,
Creating a scene that was truly unseen.
Each wall bore stories of our grand schemes,
Though our art looked like it came from bad dreams.

With giggles and goof ups, we laughed through it all,
Each canvas a chronicle, a colorful sprawl.
Our dreams on the wall, dripping and wild,
We wished for the wisdom of a grown-up child.

And as the sun dipped, our brushes lay still,
We packed up our treasures with creative thrill.
In hues of joy, our laughter remained,
An art gallery filled with fun uncontained.

Painting Memories with Barefoot Strokes

Barefoot and carefree, we raced through the grass,
With laughter that echoed, like shadows they'd pass.
Our feet were our brushes, the ground was our canvas,
Each print a reminder of fun we'd amass.

The grass tickled toes, like secrets they'd tell,
Of leaps and of bounds, a youthful spell.
We'd slide down the hills, a messy brigade,
With mud on our faces, our childhood parade.

Puddles were oceans, our boots left behind,
We transformed into dolphins with just a kind mind.
Each splash was a giggle, each giggle a cheer,
Honoring dreams that once felt so near.

And when the sun set, we shelved our delight,
But memories lingered, like stars in the night.
With barefooted strokes, we painted our way,
A masterpiece born of wild, joyful play.

Sipping Sunshine, Storing Memories

We'd sit on the steps with our lemonade cups,
Counting the clouds and the hiccuping pups.
Sipping on sunshine, we'd chat and conspire,
Creating grand worlds that never grew tiresome.

With straws like rockets, we launched all our dreams,
While sticky sweet fingers unfolded the schemes.
Each sip was a giggle, each gulp was a tale,
As summer drifted by on a glorious sail.

The ice in our drinks danced like children, carefree,
Melting away as we argued in glee.
Our laughter spilled over, our secrets like rain,
We were kings and queens of our playful domain.

And as twilight whispered, we made one last toast,
To memories made and the friendships we boast.
With each tiny sip, we captured the glow,
Of a sunshine-filled world that we'd lovingly stow.

Captured Moments in the Summer Air

In the yard, we played with glee,
Catching fireflies, wild and free.
Sneaking snacks from mom's great stash,
With a giggle and a sudden crash.

Lemonade spills on the warm grass,
We dare each other, we're all sass.
Silly faces, marshmallow fights,
Chasing shadows on starry nights.

Old bikes racing down the street,
Pedal fast, don't miss a beat!
Flip-flops flying, laughter rings,
Oh, the joy that summer brings!

In the sunsets, our dreams unfold,
Tiny secrets we dare not hold.
With whispered plans beneath the moon,
Silly songs that end too soon.

Memories Weaved in the Fabric of Time

Socks on feet, we slide in style,
In the hallway, we run a mile.
On rain-soaked nights, we splash and splash,
With rubber ducks in a crazy dash.

Grandma's stories, wacky and wild,
She says we're just her favorite child.
Tales of pirates, and treasure maps,
And noodle fights that end in claps.

Friday nights with popcorn galore,
Binge-watching shows and wanting more.
Every giggle felt like a prize,
With silly dances that made us rise.

With all these moments sewn in a line,
Time thinks we're silly, but we feel fine.
Each glance, each smile, forever stays,
In our hearts where laughter plays.

Laughter that Danced in the Evening

The evening glow with warmth and cheer,
We spin around, without a fear.
Jumping in puddles, soaking wet,
With every laugh, no time to fret.

Tickle fights and sneaky grins,
Competing in games and silly spins.
Chasing dreams under the twinkling light,
Making shadows that took flight.

Late-night crickets sing their tune,
We whisper secrets under the moon.
Branching out in fun, oh what a sight,
Every moment feels just right.

In our hearts, these laughs remain,
Echoes of joy in every vein.
With time standing still, we'll always be,
The silly kids we were, carefree.

Sunsets Over the Childhood Lane

With paint-stained hands, we ran so fast,
Creating memories meant to last.
Every sunset brings a brand new spark,
As we dance and play till it's dark.

Crickets chirping in a joyful tone,
As we tell tales, never alone.
Chasing the night, we set the pace,
Giggling through time, a happy race.

Daydreams flutter like leaves in flight,
Sprinkling laughter in the fading light.
With ice cream drips and candy mounds,
The echo of joy forever resounds.

In these moments, we felt so grand,
In every whisper, in every hand.
As the stars peek through the playful sky,
We'll hold onto youth, as the days fly by.

www.ingramcontent.com/pod-product-compliance
Lightning Source LLC
Chambersburg PA
CBHW060129230426
43661CB00003B/369